USING THIS BOOK

*Children learn to read by **reading**, but they need help to begin with.*

When you have read the story on the left-hand pages aloud to the child, go back to the beginning of the book and look at the pictures together.

Encourage children to read the sentences under the pictures. If they don't know a word, give them a chance to 'guess' what it is from the illustrations, before telling them.

There are more suggestions for helping children to learn to read in the *Parent/Teacher* booklet.

British Library Cataloguing in Publication Data

McCullagh, Sheila K.
    Mr. Grimble grumbles. —(Puddle Lane).
    1. Readers—*1950-*
    I. Title   II. Aitchison, Martin   III. Series
    428.6   PE1119
    ISBN 0-7214-1017-0

First edition

Published by Ladybird Books Ltd Loughborough Leicestershire UK
Ladybird Books Inc Lewiston Maine 04240 USA

Printed in England

Mr Grimble grumbles

written by SHEILA McCULLAGH
illustrated by MARTIN AITCHISON

This book belongs to:

Ladybird Books

Mr and Mrs Grimble lived in Puddle Lane.
Mrs Grimble was always very cheerful,
but Mr Grimble wasn't.
He was always grumbling.
He began to grumble as soon as
he got up in the morning,
and he went on grumbling all day.
He was still grumbling
when he went to bed at night.

Mr Grimble began to grumble
as soon as he got up.

One day, he began to grumble
even more than usual.
He grumbled about his breakfast.
His tea was too hot, and
his toast was too cold.
One egg was too hard, and
the other too soft.
He grumbled and grumbled and grumbled.

Mr Grimble grumbled
and grumbled and grumbled.

"Why don't you go out?"
asked Mrs Grimble.
"It's a very fine day."

"I don't want to go out," said Mr Grimble.

"Then stay in, and I'll make you
another cup of tea," said Mrs Grimble.

"I don't want to stay in," said Mr Grimble.
"I'll go out."
He put on his boots, but
his bootlace broke.
He put on his hat, but
his hat fell off, so
he grumbled and grumbled and grumbled.

Mr Grimble grumbled
and grumbled and grumbled.

He tied his bootlace.
He picked up his hat.
He took his stick and
went out into Puddle Lane.
Sarah and Davy, Hari and Gita
were all in the lane, playing hop-scotch.
"What a noise you all make!"
grumbled Mr Grimble. "I do wish
I could have some peace and quiet!"

Mr Grimble went out
into Puddle Lane.

He went off down the lane,
grumbling to himself.
As he came to the archway
leading to Market Square,
he met the Magician.
"Good morning, Mr Grimble,"
said the Magician.

"It may be a good morning for **you**.
It isn't a good morning for **me**,"
said Mr Grimble. "**You're** a Magician.
You can do anything you like.
I only wish **I** was a Magician."

Mr Grimble went down
the lane.
He met the Magician.
"I wish I was a magician,"
said Mr Grimble.

"Well, I can't turn you into a magician,"
said the Magician. "But I can
give you a wish. The next time
you wish for anything, it will happen."
The Magician snapped his fingers.
"Remember," he said,
"You can have one wish.
You can't wish to be a magician,
but you can wish for anything else.
So be careful what you wish for."
The Magician went on his way,
up Puddle Lane.

"You can't be a magician,
but I will give you a wish,"
said the Magician.

"It's not much use having a wish, if
I can't use it to become a magician,"
grumbled Mr Grimble.
"If I can't be a magician,
I'm not going to wish for anything."
He looked out into Market Square,
but he didn't see anyone,
so he turned around, and
went back up Puddle Lane,
grumbling as he went.

Mr Grimble went back
up Puddle Lane.

The children were still playing in the lane.
"I need peace and quiet,"
muttered Mr Grimble.
And he went through the gates,
into the Magician's garden.

Mr Grimble went into
the Magician's garden.

The first thing he saw was the Griffle.
The Griffle was standing under a tree,
with his back to him.
Mr Grimble hadn't seen the Griffle before,
and he was rather frightened.
"Go away!" he cried, waving his stick.
"Go away!"

Mr Grimble saw the Griffle.
"Go away!" he cried.
"Go away!"

The Griffle turned round.
He saw Mr Grimble, and vanished.
"Well, that's a strange thing!"
said Mr Grimble.
"A vanishing monster!
I only wish **I** could vanish like that,
when I see someone I don't want
to talk to."

The Griffle saw Mr Grimble,
and vanished.
''I wish I could vanish,''
said Mr Grimble.

But as soon as he said,
"I wish I could vanish,"
Mr Grimble vanished.
There was nothing left of him
to be seen, but his boots,
and his stick, and his hat!

As soon as he said,
"I wish I could vanish,"
Mr Grimble vanished.

Mr Grimble looked at his hand.

"Where's it gone?" he cried.

"I can't see it."

He looked down at his leg

but his leg had vanished.

All he could see, were his boots.

"What's happened?" he cried.

"Whatever has happened to me?"

Then he remembered that the Magician

had given him one wish.

"I do believe I've vanished!"

cried Mr Grimble. "Whatever shall I do?"

Mr Grimble looked down
at his leg,
but his leg had vanished.

Mr Grimble turned,
and hurried back home.
Mrs Grimble heard the front door open.
"Come in," she called.
"You're just in time for a cup of tea."
Mr Grimble went into the kitchen.
At least, his hat and his boots
and his stick went into the kitchen.
Mr Grimble was there, too,
but Mrs Grimble couldn't see him.

Mr Grimble went in.
Mrs Grimble could see his hat,
his boots and his stick,
but she couldn't see Mr Grimble.

Poor Mrs Grimble got such a shock,
that she dropped the tea cup.
"Whatever is it?" cried Mrs Grimble.
"Whatever can it be?"

"It's only me," said Mr Grimble,
sitting down heavily in a chair.
"I met the Magician in the lane,
and he gave me a wish.
He said I could wish for anything I liked."

"Do you mean you wished
you could vanish?" asked Mrs Grimble.
"Whyever would you wish
a thing like that?"

"I met the Magician,"
said Mr Grimble.
"The Magician gave me
a wish."

"I didn't mean to," said Mr Grimble.
"I saw a monster in the Magician's garden.
The monster vanished –
and I wished I could vanish, too.
I forgot the Magician had given me
a wish. Whatever shall I do?"

"I wished I could vanish,"
said Mr Grimble.

"Go and see the Magician at once,"
said Mrs Grimble. "He'll help you.
You can't go about like that."

"I'll go straight away," said Mr Grimble.

"I'll have a cup of tea ready,
when you get back," said Mrs Grimble.

"I shall need it," said Mr Grimble.
The chair creaked.
Mrs Grimble saw the boots and the hat
and the stick go out of the room.
She heard the front door open and close.
Mrs Grimble shook her head.
"I wonder if he'll ever learn,"
she said to herself.

"Go and see the Magician,"
said Mrs Grimble.
She saw the boots
and the stick
and the hat go out.

The Magician was coming out of his house,
when Mr Grimble came into the garden.
He looked at the boots and the hat
and the stick, and he guessed
what had happened.
He laughed.

"Well, Mr Grimble," said the Magician.
"I didn't think you would want
to become invisible!"

"I don't," said Mr Grimble.
"I didn't mean to make that wish.
It slipped out. Help me!
I want to be myself again,
just as I was before. Help me!
Please help me!"

"Very well, I will," said the Magician.

Mr Grimble met the Magician
in the Magician's garden.

"Help me!" said Mr Grimble.

"I will," said the Magician.

He snapped his fingers —
and there was Mr Grimble.
Mr Grimble was himself again.
He looked at his hand.
He could see it.
He could see his legs, too.
Mr Grimble looked at the Magician.
"Thank you," he said.
"Thank you, Magician."

It was the first time Mr Grimble
had said thank you to anyone for years.

"Thank you," said Mr Grimble.
"Thank you, Magician."

When Mr Grimble got home,
Mrs Grimble gave him a cup of tea.
"Thank you," said Mr Grimble.
"I needed that."
Mrs Grimble was so surprised, that
she almost dropped the cup again.

And after that, although Mr Grimble
still grumbled from time to time,
he didn't grumble nearly as much
as he had grumbled before.
And he was **much** more careful about
what he said.

Mrs Grimble gave Mr Grimble
a cup of tea.
"Thank you," said Mr Grimble.

Notes for the parent/teacher

When you have read the story, go back to the beginning. Look at each picture and talk about it, pointing to the caption below, and reading it aloud yourself.

Run your finger along under the words as you read, so that the child learns that reading goes from left to right. (You needn't say this in so many words. Children learn many useful things about reading by just reading with you, and it is often better to let them learn by experience, rather than by explanation.) When you next go through the book, encourage the child to read the words and sentences under the illustrations.

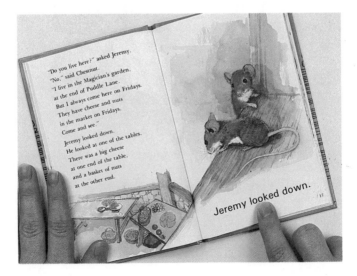

Don't rush in with the word before she* has time to think, but don't leave her struggling for too long. Always encourage her to feel that she is reading successfully, praising her when she does well, and avoiding criticism.

Now turn back to the beginning, and print the child's name in the space on the *title page, using ordinary, not capital letters. Let her watch you print it: this is another useful experience.*

Children enjoy hearing the same story many times. Read this one as often as the child likes hearing it. The more opportunities she has of looking at the illustrations and **reading** *the captions with you, the more she will come to recognise the words. Don't worry if she* **remembers** *rather than* **reads** *the captions. This is a normal stage in learning.*

If you have a number of books, let her choose which story she would like to have again.

**Footnote:* In order to avoid the continual "he or she", "him or her", the child is referred to in this book as "she". However, the stories are equally appropriate to boys and girls.

Have you read these stories about the Magician in Puddle Lane?

Stage 1

Stage 2

*from
Danger! Dragon!*

from Tim turns green